Super Explorers

CASTLES & KNIGHTS

Tamara Hartson

What is a Castle?

Egeskov Castle, Denmark

A castle is a building that was made to hold off attacks by invaders. Castles were the homes of noblemen or royalty. People built castles for over a thousand years and on every continent except Antarctica.

Most castles were built during the Middle Ages. Nowadays, castles are museums or heritage sites. Only a few have people living in them.

Parts of a Castle

Bailey (Courtyard)

Battlements

Gatehouse

Defensive Towers

Keep

Arrowslits

Defensive Tower

Curtain Wall

Castles were mainly built of stone and wood. Stone was shaped by hand using chisels and hammers. It took hundreds of men from 2 to 10 years to build a single castle.

The people who built castles had special skills. There were carpenters, masons (stone workers), diggers, quarrymen and blacksmiths, all working under the master builder. The master builder was like the architect of a castle.

Building a Castle

Stone had to be moved from a quarry to the building site. Once a stone was at the building site, masons chiseled it into the right shape before fitting it into the wall with mortar (cement).

Curtain Wall

The **curtain wall** may have defensive towers at the corners or in the middle. The walls and towers usually have **battlements** and **arrowslits**.

Carcassonne, France

Some castles have a single curtain wall, and some castles have two, one inside the other, for extra protection from invaders. This castle has two! The central area inside the wall is called the bailey.

Keep

Château de Vincennes, France

Most castles have a keep. The keep is a tower within the curtain wall that is the home of the nobleman or king.

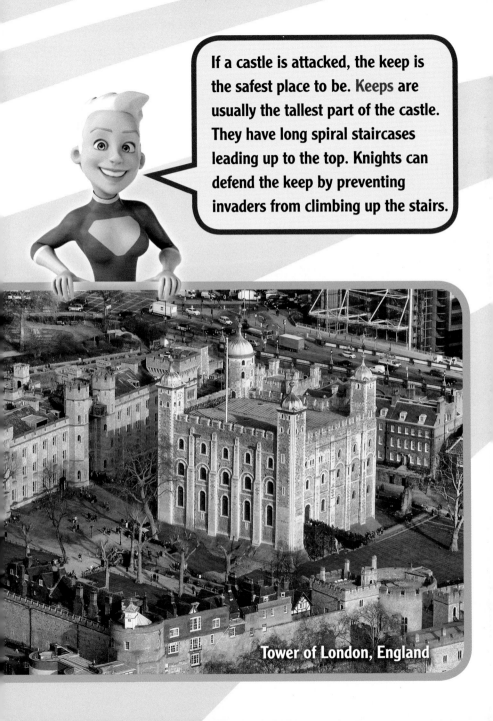

If a castle is attacked, the keep is the safest place to be. **Keeps** are usually the tallest part of the castle. They have long spiral staircases leading up to the top. Knights can defend the keep by preventing invaders from climbing up the stairs.

Tower of London, England

Motte and Bailey

Motte

Bailey

Model of York Castle, England

The motte is either surrounded by the bailey and curtain wall, or it is surrounded by a moat.

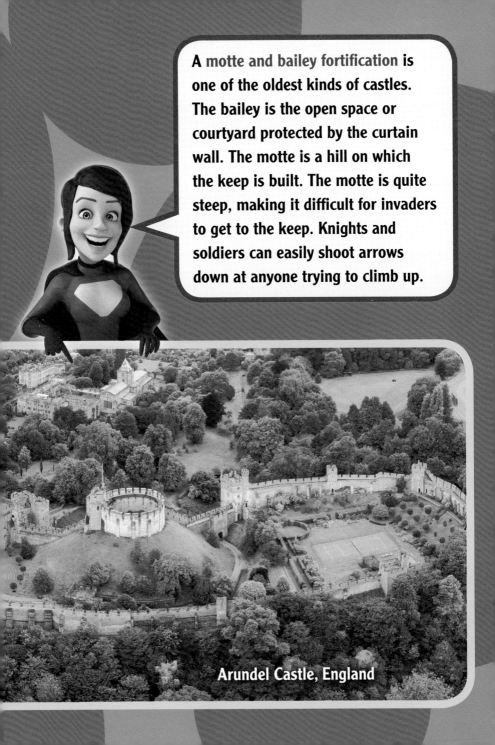

A **motte and bailey fortification** is one of the oldest kinds of castles. The bailey is the open space or courtyard protected by the curtain wall. The motte is a hill on which the keep is built. The motte is quite steep, making it difficult for invaders to get to the keep. Knights and soldiers can easily shoot arrows down at anyone trying to climb up.

Arundel Castle, England

Gatehouse

Bishop's Palace, England

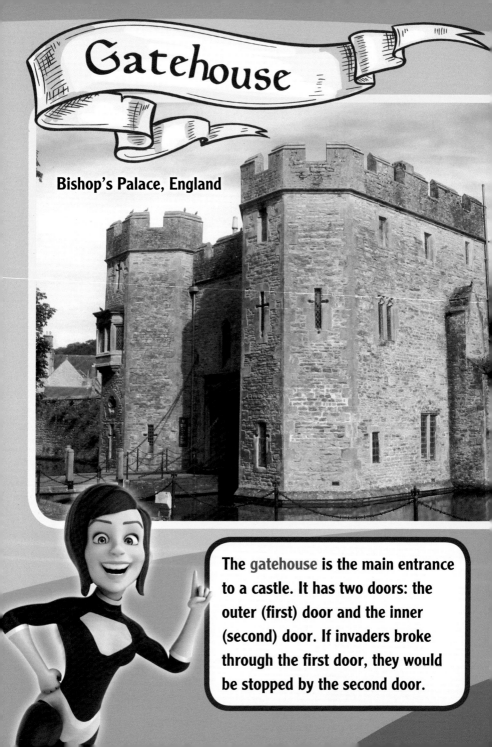

The gatehouse is the main entrance to a castle. It has two doors: the outer (first) door and the inner (second) door. If invaders broke through the first door, they would be stopped by the second door.

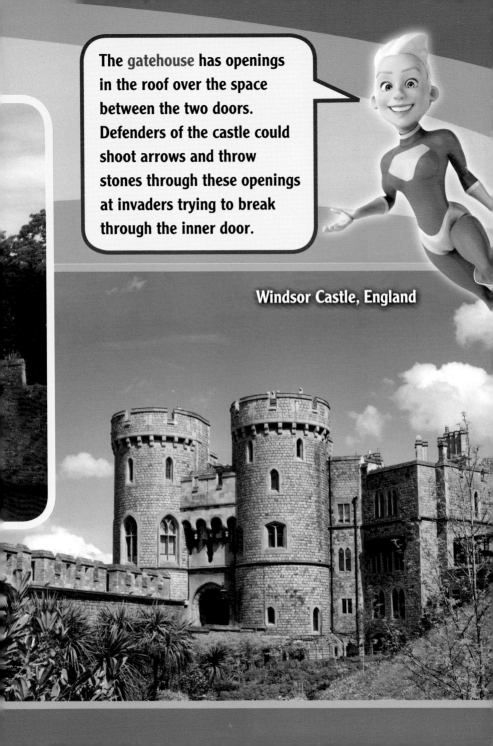

The **gatehouse** has openings in the roof over the space between the two doors. Defenders of the castle could shoot arrows and throw stones through these openings at invaders trying to break through the inner door.

Windsor Castle, England

Moat

Caerlaverock Castle, Scotland

Some castles had water-filled moats. Making moats was difficult and could only be done where there was enough water. The moat protected the castle by making it difficult for invaders to attack the curtain wall.

Bodiam Castle, England

A moat stopped invaders from putting a seige tower against the curtain wall. The moat also prevented people from digging a tunnel under the wall.

Drawbridge

A **drawbridge** is a **movable bridge** that crosses over a castle's moat. Chains or ropes attached to the bridge allow it to be lifted up.

Drawbridges were left down in peace time to allow people to enter and exit the castle. When the castle was attacked, the drawbridge was raised to prevent invaders from crossing the moat.

When a drawbridge was pulled up, it blocked the gatehouse door, adding another layer of protection.

Portcullis

The main entrance to a castle was usually defended with a portcullis. This is a special kind of sliding door or gate that was made of strong wood or iron.

Battlements & Arrowslits

The **battlements** are the top part of the curtain wall. They protect a walkway. Gaps in the battlements allowed archers to fire arrows at invaders.

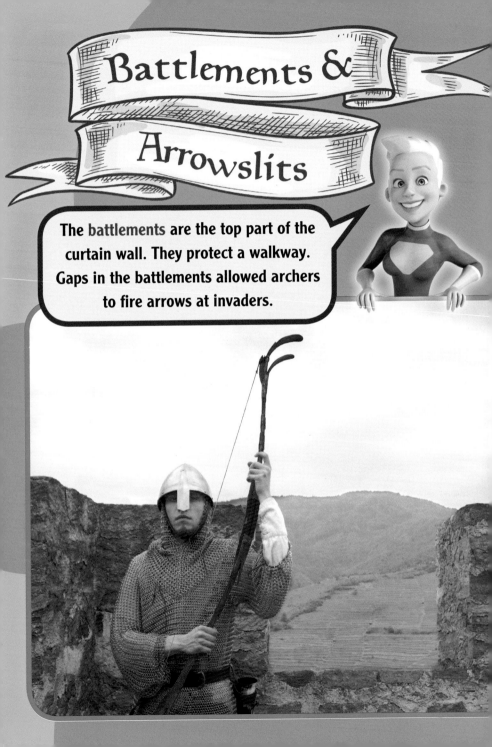

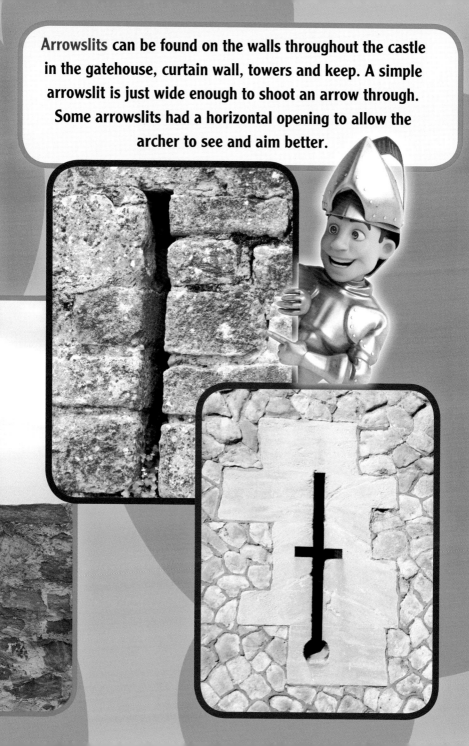

Arrowslits can be found on the walls throughout the castle in the gatehouse, curtain wall, towers and keep. A simple arrowslit is just wide enough to shoot an arrow through. Some arrowslits had a horizontal opening to allow the archer to see and aim better.

Stairways

Castle stairways **were typically narrow and steep, and they spiraled up to the right. This** meant that invaders had to go up one at at time, usually carrying a sword in their right hand against the central pillar. Defenders, on the other hand, could swing their swords easily from above.

Staircases were also often built with uneven stairs. People who lived in the castle knew the stairs and could run up or down them easily. Invaders who were unfamiliar with the stairs were more likely to trip and fall.

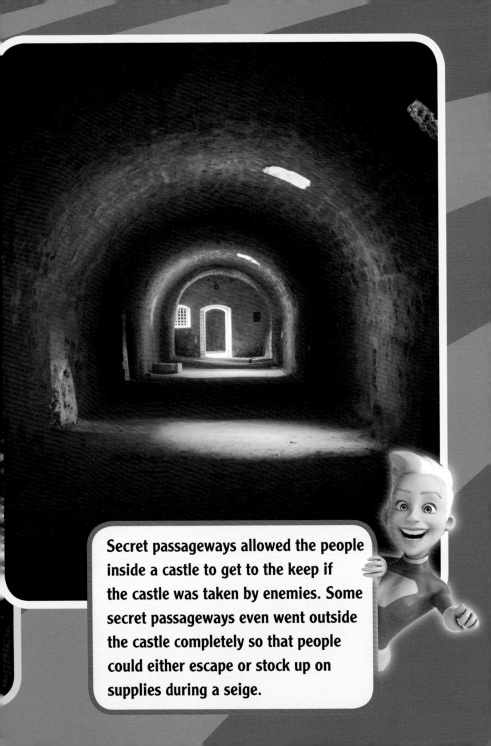

Secret passageways allowed the people inside a castle to get to the keep if the castle was taken by enemies. Some secret passageways even went outside the castle completely so that people could either escape or stock up on supplies during a seige.

Dungeons

Captured invaders and criminals were sometimes held in dungeons. Dungeons were underground beneath the castle. They were always cold, dark and damp.

Prisoners were kept in the dungeon either chained to the wall or held behind metal bars.

Inside a Castle

The lighting inside a castle came from torches and candles because there was no electricity. The person who made the candles was called a chandler. People throughout the castle had to light candles each morning.

Castles may have been beautiful, but they weren't very comfortable. Most castles were cold. Fireplaces heated the castle. Only the most important rooms had fireplaces.

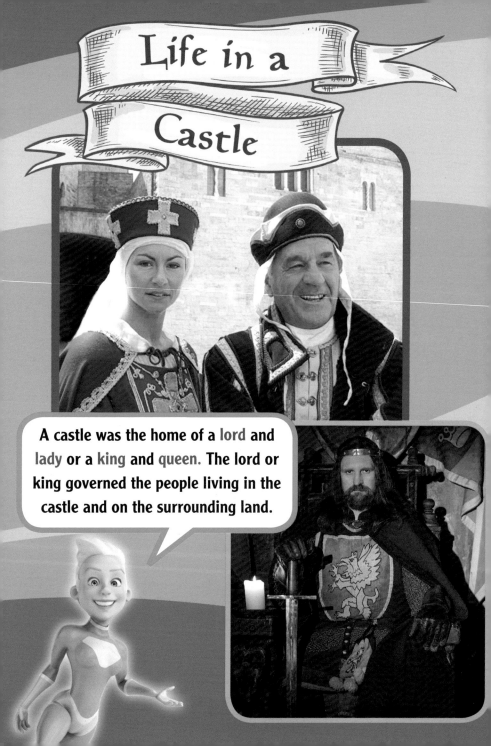

Life in a

Castle

A castle was the home of a lord and lady or a king and queen. The lord or king governed the people living in the castle and on the surrounding land.

The people who lived in the castle had jobs:
- the chamberlain ran the household,
- the chambermaids tidied the bedrooms, and
- the butler managed wine and food service.

Other castle staff included the cooks, chandler, blacksmith and armorers.

Knight

A **knight** was a man (sometimes a woman) who swore allegiance to his king or lord. This meant he had to fight in battles and defend the castle. He was given gold and property to pay for his skills.

Armor

Plate armor offered the most protection for a knight. Joints in the metal allowed a knight to bend and move. A full suit of armor weighed as much as a 4-year-old child and was hot! Wearing armor was safe but not very comfortable!

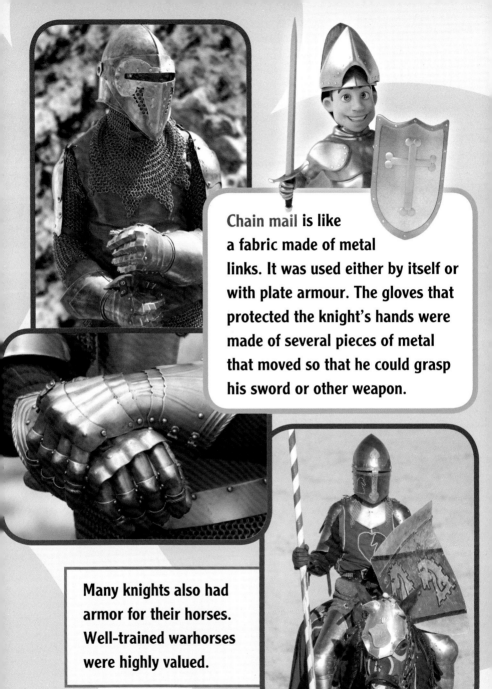

Chain mail is like a fabric made of metal links. It was used either by itself or with plate armour. The gloves that protected the knight's hands were made of several pieces of metal that moved so that he could grasp his sword or other weapon.

Many knights also had armor for their horses. Well-trained warhorses were highly valued.

Weapons

A knight used many types of weapons. His main weapon was a sword with a shield to protect his body. Knights were also skilled at archery.

Bow and Quiver of Arrows

Other weapons included axes, maces and spears. Blacksmiths made the metal parts of all the weapons. The most skilled blacksmiths made the strongest and sharpest swords.

Flail Mace

Axes

Becoming a Knight

Becoming a knight started in boyhood. At age 7, a boy became a page and learned the rules of the court, chivalry, weapons, reading and writing. He was also an assistant to his lord or a knight.

When the boy turned 15, he became a squire.
Squires learned riding, swimming, armed
combat, wrestling, long jumping and dancing.
As a squire, a boy also assisted knights
with their armor.

Horsemanship

Knights were trained in horsemanship from an early age. A knight with excellent riding skills was highly respected.

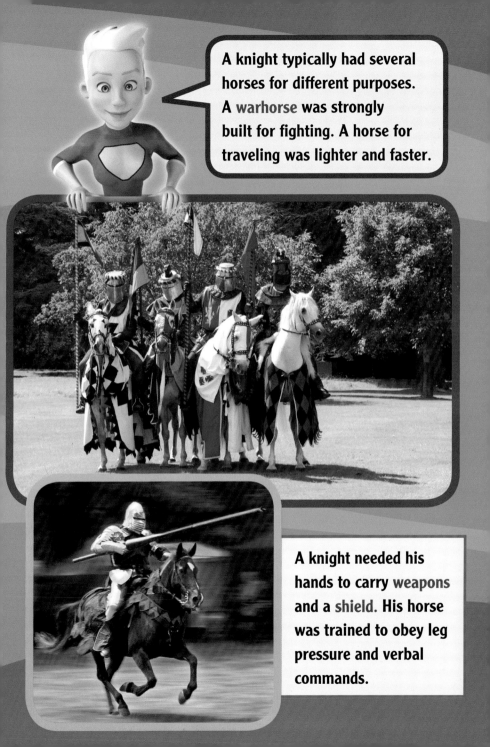

A knight typically had several horses for different purposes. A warhorse was strongly built for fighting. A horse for traveling was lighter and faster.

A knight needed his hands to carry weapons and a shield. His horse was trained to obey leg pressure and verbal commands.

Heraldry

Heraldry is about creating and displaying coats of arms. The colors and coat of arms a knight wore on his armor, shield and flag showed his allegiance.

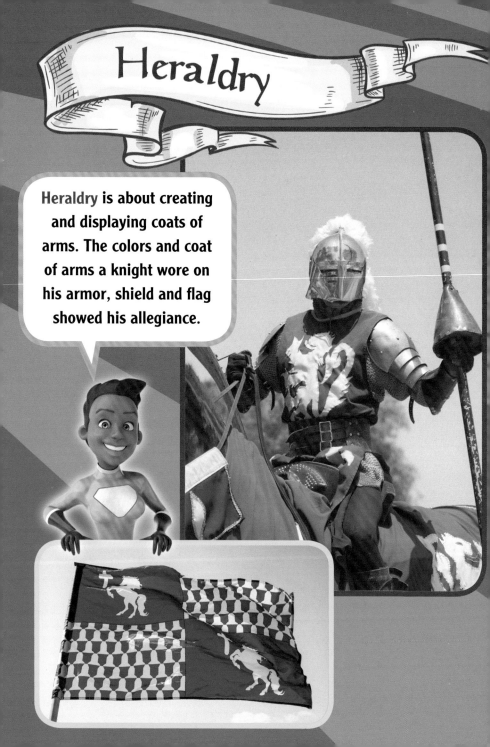

Tournaments

In times of peace, knights competed in tournaments. Competitions included battles called melees, where knights fought with swords until only the winner was left standing.

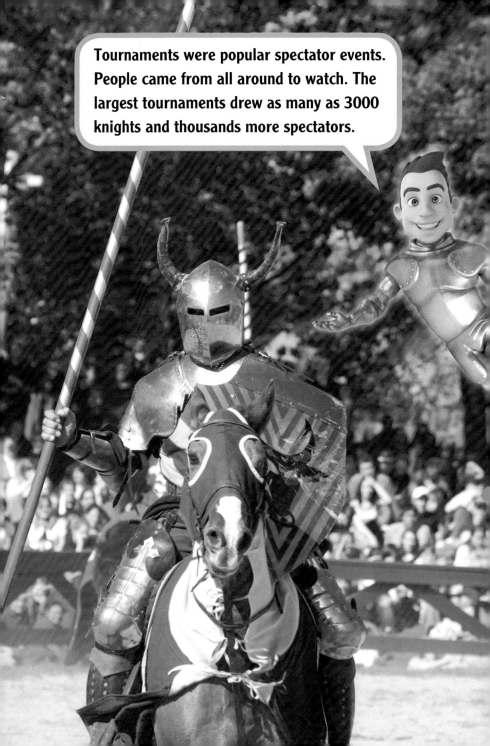

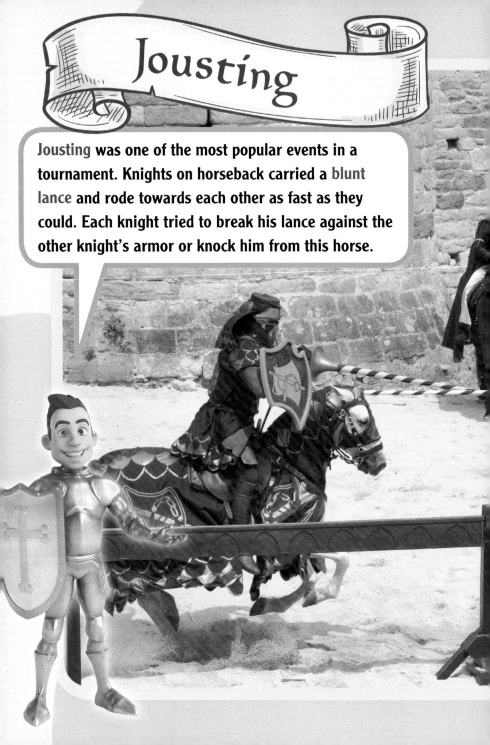

Jousting

Jousting was one of the most popular events in a tournament. Knights on horseback carried a blunt lance and rode towards each other as fast as they could. Each knight tried to break his lance against the other knight's armor or knock him from this horse.

The loser had to turn his horse and armor over to the winning knight.

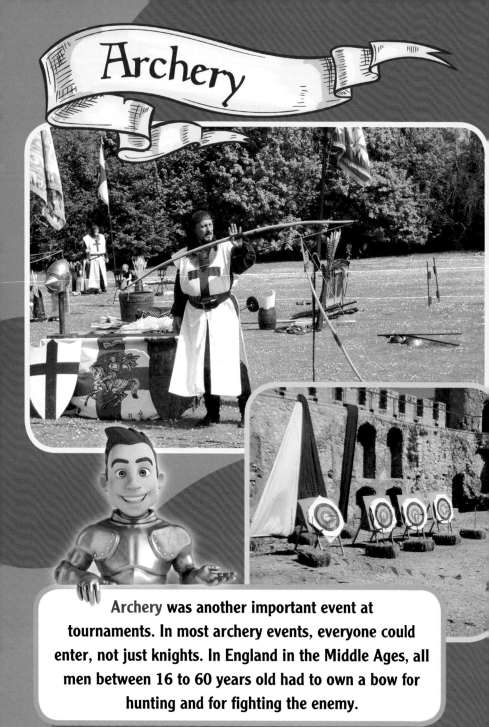

Archery

Archery was another important event at tournaments. In most archery events, everyone could enter, not just knights. In England in the Middle Ages, all men between 16 to 60 years old had to own a bow for hunting and for fighting the enemy.

Knights also practiced using arrows that were dipped in oil and lit on fire. If knights attacked a fortress made of wood, fire arrows could cause a lot of damage.

Dragons

Legends from the Middle Ages told of great, fire-breathing **dragons** that lived in abandoned castles. They guarded vast treasures of gold and silver.

Battles

The most successful and experienced knights were chosen as the leaders. When knights went into battle, their leader was the strongest and most decorated knight.

Melee fighting is when knights and other soldiers battled each other at close quarters. Battles were fought to conquer new territory and defeat invading armies.

Attacking a Castle

Castles were built to withstand attacks, so many tools and weapons were invented to attack them. The seige tower was like a covered staircase or ladder that could be wheeled against the castle wall. Soldiers could then climb up safely and enter the castle.

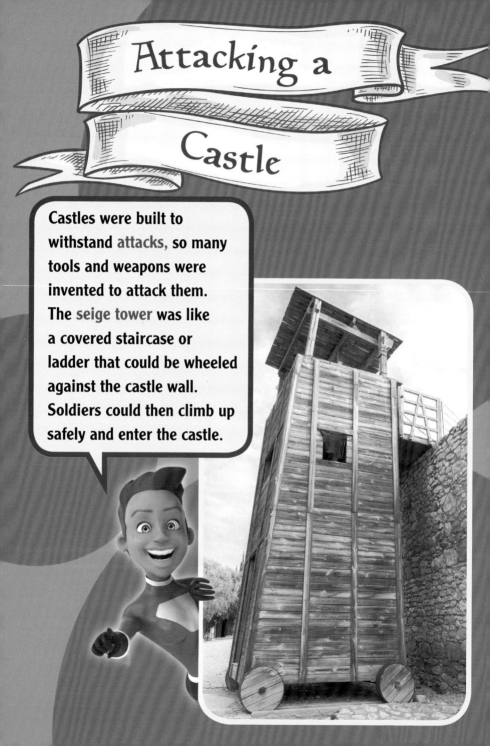

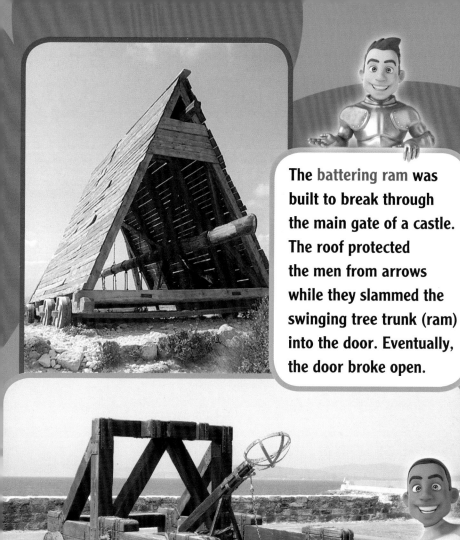

The battering ram was built to break through the main gate of a castle. The roof protected the men from arrows while they slammed the swinging tree trunk (ram) into the door. Eventually, the door broke open.

There were many kinds of catapults used during the Middle Ages. Catapults could throw rocks or flaming projectiles into a castle, killing people and weakening the castle walls.

Downfall of
Castles & Knights

Castles were the best defensive buildings for hundreds of years. When cannons became common, castles became less important. Cannons were powerful enough to destroy a castle in a short time. A single cannonball fired with gunpowder could knock down a castle wall and allow invading soldiers to enter.

Crossbow

The downfall of knights occurred as weapons became more powerful and easier to use. Crossbows could be fired by anyone without special training. The bolt (arrow) could pierce a knight's armor. Later, firearms made it even easier for untrained soldiers to defend against knights. Medieval knights, even in armor, could not compete against gunpowder and guns.

Other Kinds of Castles

Castles were built in many countries, not just in Europe. Castles in other parts of the world looked very different.

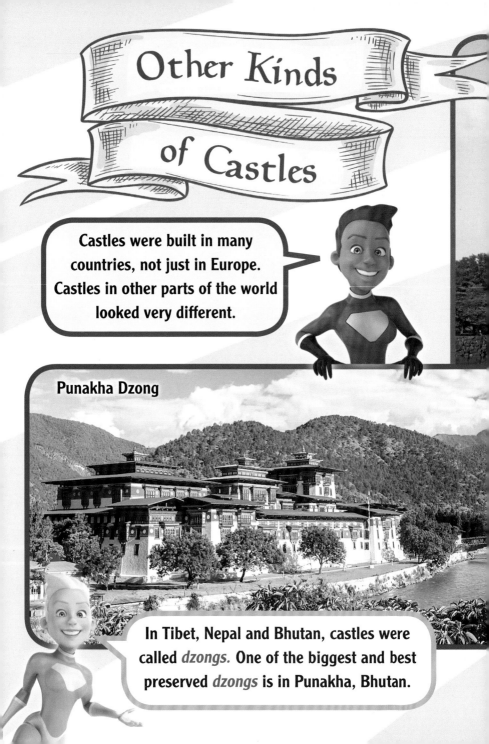

Punakha Dzong

In Tibet, Nepal and Bhutan, castles were called *dzongs.* One of the biggest and best preserved *dzongs* is in Punakha, Bhutan.

Matsumoto Castle, Japan

Matsumoto Castle in Japan is one the country's best preserved castles. It has a gatehouse, a keep, three baileys, two towers and a moat. In Japan, the trained warriors, called *samurai,* protected a castle and swore allegiance to a *daimyo* (lord).

Famous Castles

Warwick Castle,
England

Edinburgh Castle, Scotland

Himeji Castle, Japan

Neuschwanstein Castle, Germany

Citadel, Egypt

Windsor Castle, England

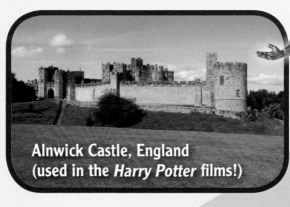

Alnwick Castle, England
(used in the *Harry Potter* films!)

© 2018 Super Explorers

Printed in China

All rights reserved. No part of this work covered by the copyrights hereon may be reproduced or used in any form or by any means—graphic, electronic or mechanical—without the prior written permission of the publisher, except for reviewers, who may quote brief passages. Any request for photocopying, recording, taping or storage on information retrieval systems of any part of this work shall be directed in writing to the publisher.

The Publisher: Super Explorers is an imprint of Blue Bike Books

Library and Archives Canada Cataloguing in Publication

Hartson, Tamara, 1974–, author
    Castles & knights / Tamara Hartson.

Issued in print and electronic formats.
ISBN 978-1-926700-98-4 (softcover)
ISBN 978-1-926700-99-1 (EPUB)

    1. Castles—Miscellanea—Juvenile literature. 2. Knights and knighthood—Miscellanea—Juvenile literature. 3. Civilization, Medieval—Miscellanea—Juvenile literature. I. Title. II. Title: Castles and knights.

GT3550.H38 2019	j940.1	C2018-905981-8
		C2018-905982-6

Front cover credit: From Getty Images: Anna_Brothankova, NejroN, Mustang_79.

Back cover credits: From Getty Images: Gannet77, alessandroguerriero, tamara_kulikova.

Photo Credits: Anne Robichaud (www.annesitaly.com, www.stayassisi.com), 32a. From Getty Images: 1amgreen, 14; AlamarPhotography, 15; alessandroguerriero, 34-35; Anna Egorova, 6; Argestes, 49a; balhash, 44b; bcreigh, 43b; Bertl123, 62b; Besjunior, 31; bogonet, 58; delray77, 45a; Demid, 46; denis_t, 39b; DeSid, 27; dja65, 38a; Dmitriy Bezzubenko, 39c; DorukTR, 30a; Dougfir, 37c; ehrlif, 26; Emilija Randjelovic, 39a; FairytaleDesign, 29b; flowersandclassicalmusic, 43a; fotofrankyat, 22, 51a; Fotografiapau, 24a; fotokostic, 52-53; friedmanwd, 17; Gannet77, 42; Geerati, 4-5; gsermek, 37a; GuyGentry, 20a; HenkBentlage, 37b; javarman3, 9-10; johnnorth, 19a; Kilav, 45b; lemonpink, 33a; llitten, 47; MarinaMariya, 25; MortenElm, 2-3; NejroN, 38b; nikicruz, 28; Nobilior, 30b; noimagination, 59; PlazacCameraman, 23a; prestongeorge, 57b; puchan, 54-55; ratpack223, 36; RTsubin, 21; Sabine Hortebusch, 60; scanrail, 24b; stanzi11, 20b; TonyBaggett, 23b; Windzepher, 44a. From Wikimedia Commons: 663highland, 61a; Ahmed Al.Badawy, 63b; Alistair Young, 41b; Chensiyuan, 13; ChrisO, 57a; DeFacto, 62a; Diliff, 63c; Dr.Haus, 63d; Duncan, 11; Georges Jansoone, 18; Harrie Gielen, 49-50; ignis, 10; JC Hervé, 19b; Lazy KATT, 41a; Malcolm Carruthers, 33b; Martijn vdS, 33c; Medievalna, 51b; Niko Kitsakis, 62c; Ronny Siegel, 6; Ronny Siegel, 7; Simon Ledingham, 16; Stephane Gaudry, 40; Stephen Montgomery created the original, hchc2009 edited the background, 12; Superchilum, 50b; SzlakPiastowski, 54b; The Local People Photo Archive, 50a; Thomas Wolf, www.foto-tw.de, 63a; Tsungam, 29a. From 123RF: Eugene Sergeev, 56; NejroN, 32b; Yurii Hnidets, 61b.

Superhero Illustrations: julos/Thinkstock.

Text Banners: seamartini/Getty Images

Produced with the assistance of the Government of Alberta.

Alberta
Government

We acknowledge the financial support of the Government of Canada.
Nous reconnaissons l'appui financier du gouvernement du Canada.

Funded by the Government of Canada.
Financé par le gouvernement du Canada.

Canadä

PC: 38